SUN SHELTER GRAY

J. Gordon Faylor

Zahir Editions
2022

Cover images: Patricia L. Boyd, *From Before (IX, X)*, 2021
ISBN: 978-1-958158-00-5

for Emily Martin and Derek Baron

Pretending faith remonstrance
moral degrees flora clamber stalks

"obtain" strength of wind by spokes
incredible Hangar bag, bare time, clods'
groaning mouths unbearable cry favor

tensions between cricket and housefly

flagging hands Commemorate fly

cavernous touch of sweet forgiveness

Complete clues without attachments
as premise begs. General complaints
velocity moon in Trench rats around!

a relic of your past

find a professional who can't unfeel
the kinks of their trade

dose
self-defeating without fear, curse
for crinkling
a sliced bag of potatoes
rolling around in a circlular
packet "I need comparative reprieve"

collated and inferred from overboard
Internal organs of spies and dragons

lead the table to the door
lazy disarray in troubling fires
doesn't guarantee the thumb the hand

lemming "crickets"

Time to write spectacular asymmetry
No need to know cross-hairs
found first watch or security personnel

Copper furnaces smoke showers "tend"
a building that has gone away

Climb to give each other
sear of taste, dust soup chickens
a long time across town now interred

Bent at an interview with Ambidextrous
soldier-god "glossy" with make recall-mercy
plaintive wanderer comic
struck dry in conviction to sink.

There's heaven's platform, circus clown.

Recalled too from that business animal,
Desperately immersive
"Screen My Suspension" viewing
in
terror

fervent
accord dogs
of cricket, fly alike
the ark

Hath flesh nightskids
bemoaned Felicitas:
prick craters in those buildings

Climb to gift each other
Diagonal plays crash as "scruples"
desperately drawn slices thumb off

immersion
pup groans
faux ami spent
day tracked further accord
a crush's oblique play with blades

Worry at Ante Cumber
I used a false friend
chased and awakened
to liquid day

Locked door lights
I love your sunflowers
I love your sunflowers so

panel mode
Quartz wooden bellpo
wrings cornucopia
from ark's deck
it's sunset

Would animal business surf anywhere
as well on the pan of a lute?

No

Must be indignant with the cesspool
sky
Hanging ship's bell
Rattling betrayal

Screen Midnight Felicitous

Agreed

Planetary self-versus chemprop
mutant heat years as a swamp
Incidence and ridicule into
Cluttered fruit, cut and pince

Shape your wars'
good luck.
Cut Down the Layman's Heart

Skin surfs the skeleton
might still love you within

Bug quilts

Pay in pull form
Makeup cons the tiger its prey
handful of tort
Surprises people Wait for like candy
while I get to go sleep peacefully

sketch

fun while you're here, worry while you're away

Pressure imagines pain
Coloring leaves

paint the stem
trees a dirty shop tight
counts for nil, spider.

the way they ossify the mind
doesn't

Thank you cat from the back room. For meowing
flames Plush blanket death

Cut off the water hills
Used by people to die hallow
Suffocate the following facts
of their. Mortuary

"don't try to whip this poor demure" air
Pain

Awkward supple
Put in full roughness
difficult
I'm not talented actually I'm insane
people late to decline wail suffocated
I can wait love I await.

Close the horrifying contact that told the entire grave
Removed from its predecessors
an eloquence severs
skyline white
median table
"we won't work plur" sketch

They were yours here
merely worth using.

insurance?

High quality food security.

Wash the dress
in an aluminum carrier

Work I've tucked away
Believe that farmyard

Finally again, back into my blanket
with the possibility of difficult problems
fuck off and surrender

People curse days with zeal
yet extract and identify nothing

Royal money distance
Detection and focus
Everyone gives up.
Bug quilt's
Too tight to sleep
free cat tonight
Felt full

Between dark brown leaves
this paint used to dart around
Paid for its shapeliness
Starving all day
Imagine that pressure is painful
as is against pressure
a tube fear contact gloss
wresting away flubbed terror.

Poor demure tiger shops
the root of surprise
feigns pain goodly
down the human stem
as high quality food

Curse it once in death
don't try to extract anything

Use the water hill as a letter of mourning
scope much rage "within" lithe turnings
bear self against indiscretions

Slimily annihilate the facts
Awkward and supple

Fortunelike possibility with suffocant furls?
Count me.

People could love you
the same way I do
maybe wasting pride.

They were all grinning

Only a handful of those people
wear their insurance like winter.

Safety,
Wash the dress red
and aluminum conduct

used late, it's never late
when you've Done your job
believed that way in the back
also the end repairs I hope

When suffering strikes
I turn to you
for your kindness

You eat your fears
propose requirements to them,
jump around a chest they crave
Worth the sea

Take one chance
On me

You closed off and threw the blanket
away never accept reprieve

The vague prompt damp
Stupidly scared of your work

"We don't do multiple jobs"

You decide Royal money,
distance gluts
Detection and focus

it's a dog's world:
Everyone gives up
Love
When you close
Our situation. I'm doing
Imminence and can manage waiting

I love you cut
An angry cape back taken scoops
through a malty prayer in your arms
I give up let's regress
two down the hatch
flustered and simplistic
primal drinks
"cats drawn from scratch"

The day I missed my enthusiasm I buckled:
inherited heartache, unbearable tremors
flush at the computer awaiting calumny
another day
Forgotten time lasts
With your dashing
Lifting the ban-flotsam
Grinning from a distance
And torching charcoal.

Sky shirt precursor
evil and stubborn fever
greedy religion

it won't release you
refrain from income
curve and decline flowers

whole grave closes "I really liked
to sketch these cats
against a white background."

Adjustable slide mount pushdown scape
Playback of median representation Playback the
present
Until the sketched shape is solidified.
Until the sketched forms stick together.
Many people shaken
Train their clad escape
and flower-loving darts

Your emotions tell me everything
like
What you disdain clearly
or what waits for you flexibly scoped

carries a lot of danger

Turning was bad to concentrate
from
someday
I can wait
until some
Oblivion lasts
Such pop Protects

I can't keep myself away from
the time you left me. Trust me

Possibility of mount cladding
Release the stop for me who loves stoma
cats grinned at from a distance
And upon a qualified landscape.

So the perilunar effect charcoals
their wary ascent toward
"language production"?

If you wear a sky shirt = the shirt of the sky
escape

evil slide evil and stubborn fever
Religion greedy begets your siblings

Release everything you are ever
forgiven with, steel your prime
Milk refrain income for luck
decline curve and darts
money pay up the forecast

Discharge a flower
shaking of many people
anger down their backs
Supple bed drama moral remonstrance
nil you preciously count your spiders.

Verdict. Tube horror plan, badness
contentment and personnel

Perceptual ring of gloss surface
Dedicated to your home.

Coma in the courtyard on the dock
tongue moonside mutant heat
Bedkin Moonkin

Given Balance Out Music
anxious

Comparison violence comparison violence

Terrifying rental payments gluttony
A world of fleeting pondering to forgive

Dialed-in stressed trolling turtle
spanks routine envy from bad rivers
can't believe how pathetic
Make "parents suffice" put them
on the road to condemnation
atop your account
permission granted stymie
I'm trying fleets of disappearances stymie

darkness petal

Resurrected are included. Unless

Everyone has strong presence
all for a Medallion and a medal on the sly.

Who else was fitted with your leering selfishness?
Metaphor, where not poke-shame your errors?

"It's worth the brunch juice I ordered..."
Muttered into my hands. Scroll

Clogged with what you owe somehow defense
Like I want money and check, or wanted
Like a child's space or an opinion's interior
flaming conceit

Method sought before You caress
mockingbirds I'll continue to work hard for?

Fortunately, yours plays
lands of darkness and healing both.

why are we garbage

Payment and forecast tracker

hot from bad nonsense
drudge before dying in "same torrid water"
Heaven of Declining Flowers

If ghost money passed tomorrow,
I'd be first in line I mean can't mean
using time and attention to listen
over how to shop up and take stock
Hangar

Desperately pulling relieves the pain of suffering.
Write a letter selfishly and dip potato chips.
It was the last paranoia we ever knew,
a cup packer on wet grass.

A voluminous scene of peregrines freighting a storm
Snow-covered valve showroom couch
Goodbye to the glitter of the ladder to get there
that tufted me against setup forestry (as I could see)

Immune to the stars wandering the call,
I don't think I'll go anywhere for a while
So it will be difficult to manage your exercise.

When to present the stars and agree to be tired
Holiday power compares to violence like love
lists from the struck hands frail veins with them
Which aviary slips into the trailer dress
to go through cars in agony

Work mishaps loosen and foresee strangers
impeding a day's labor, forsaken laypeople
among the whipfolds of my gear
without a graveyard

forgive yourself to scratch family
horology and release trusts
Wherever the plane flies, parents are enough. Was
The side where the cry is not misaligned in deep mud
brain to brain with the captor.

The plain wooden equipment is angry, leaving a fuss,
in fact as incidence their income
merely "suggests"

Shorts armed with music-pocket

scene with liquor same imperiled
showroom by falcon-cover snow

Ladder facing furniture, sides of grasshopper
in pocket wilderness
"I code see it life's premise makes mind's junk"

Plain type competes with forestry wooden slurs
the verge of languishing hurts
of all the pills love you cherish
analyze and pay my furniture face

Input generation clods
lease trust
you
immune to a fleeting star,
loosen and foresee

I don't think I'll go anywhere for a while
so forgive me my office stress
just so your luck will get difficult.

It's enough talking about friends.
Anxiety about wandering the call
gives
do you agree to horrific moves?
Manage
Holidays forgiving children's anger
Presenting stars in deep swamps
Tired shock as I take it banal.

Comparative violence *yet*
is comparative icing on the cake

the same theories of chickenry
recitals you deem fictional reward
for efforts hitherto occluded
Frail foreseeing blankish
List from the hands you hit

Which aviary slips into showroom Felicitas?

Coma in the main courtyard and work dock

rabbit-bastard to see taste

Anger left in the child

venous chamber

taste
loosened and filled with harvest crickets
of
reconnaissance bunker blue

Difficult herbal sated misery
poster torn from sky advertising
rich meal to
Landscape two orphans
conduct
double-hearted snare fur
"It's not a rabbit"
Wooly's Last Shooting Kernel
reconnaissance bunker blue

Difficult deer torn and steamed
from the wilderness elect
Hillside dyeing
Like space pulled from the sky

With a poster where the plane went and was torn up
"like" heaven's clown

Patrol Deskant Swamp
imposing sweet escape
crows surf long out of fear

Friends filled and placed in the sky
Before a boring, stable plot line
"I have to know their location"
Rent the heart out of nonsense

If you can't destroy anything just by twisting yourself
from the side into the trash heap
last wishes of happy gray petals

I was pressed against a weak door and stumbled

faith remonstrance
Whether to fold in time

Emergency colors that lamb deer should keep
Dull gray for playing on hills and cliffs

From the side of aquamarine, the virus and the lamb

Hold play

Cancel fate Of grotesque medicine
Hungry for many moves to support righteousness

Where are they sweet

Where are thy sweets
why

when safety strikes

Remember to be careful. To avoid barriers?
Anchor crystal
sacrificial and cheap,
Have everything

Tasteless dry, bunker blue's
Visualized connection stuck.

The center of the dangerous hill protect
Even if you say it's like a cliff orcs will
Cheerful trust, secret glen enemy tools
I like this: How to upload inheritance
Crow and trundle, bow and sibling
Permission to their wing-like frost
The unfortunate painter deer torn and steamed

hand of soil
trembles
escapes on the hillside imposed
clay
snowflash "convinced disaster"
whipped by plates

of those who repent there's recovery
period and the rest

Increment of hot mixed leaves of
falling yellow sky I can't contain
There is no clasp in my heart, Bedkin Moonkin
I
Assume my love abbreviated
smells sweet and robs you
of accord you laughed at.

Cruel
Double way

Borrow the bad spear of the dawn and its whelp
put yourself in using a thimble
wait on borrowing malediction
sweat chemical reprieve

Tip, trouble, depressive.

Killing time until a chance comes spelling
Please give me some of that bitten trouble
streaming down your neck and chest

I can't laugh waiting.

The circus lives heaven among
discharged flowers dogs at the ready?

Dangerous at the center broke from the storm
Reloaded pause-shot lip of the plains
crack of indecency and fiction

I sometimes if you're the only one
We won't talk to your face
told "from your face" no contact

No stress in the graveyard office today!

Everyone expressed in words separately
concept-heavy harmonic "fuss"

Ship known clock
Cagey History and Newly preferred

not the best way to get back exactly

sticky, not uncruel
your boneless anger stalked trepidation,
seized it, heavenly canine trials

I gave as much truth to our block
as broke up legitimate resuscitation—
a life of maintenance and approval.
When you give me trust
Betrayal wipes fuckwad
tropes nice

You never trusted to hear well however,
brained with a glossy prisoner-king

You could attribute good to and take on
Bad tarmac yet you never did

I'm going to join me again, once more
starts and fits pull you in
Come to me compassion

I put a bold, divergent spoon down my throat
two throats really

gloated sneaky voices from above work

I regretted that up at the fortress,
regret my time here too
ruing the dry aspersion of jail

Dry like an oak. The stop sign glows
Trying to challenge "win the dump"

I can't win because a powerhouse
couldn't mend your heart any emptier
than a chicken could its lack of contact

Why have a snare fur we should have
Adjacency when poor
Incompletely.
Incarnation of lovers' Children pray
mush trite "That's all I have" fences

hills and ocean below ferret
Canard blanco

If you think you are cautious
For this military experiment stun
recitals you consider to be fiction
Don't be shy stolen bait traffic

Fuel an unusually sociable week finally
Bent over the bunk bed and let
the roster enigma detection and focus
weigh
entangled press with military
of all people against your logic.

The writing inside gets beaten with it,
we're thrown off leaned in the corner
left to pick up the trash
"worse"
I was betrayed by a friend who left (mentally)
after accord did them promise.
Sorry
What did they do about it? The street
there was a "close" eerie quiet place, I
Looking back on the enemy's tools

It filled my time and harassments
Until I couldn't work anymore.
They
I'm so tired of treating hell
like a caliphate's red armor
gone insufferably princely.

Stem or hair swarm consultant

From the bottom of the chest
you jumped overboard

how you were worth the sea
nothing's worth that now

give them one last chance
People can love you
Just like me.

If you don't contact me, don't contact me
I'm trying to write in I can do anything
Let go of compassionate spelling
for people often people wear it

Time at the fortress thrown to the curb

Trust instead the chicken fathoms
betrayed by a friend and left
Dry like an oak pausing attempted murder
to speak onstage about conditional friendship

What am I trying to challenge and win
to find the power of happiness
Bent over the bunk bed

Have a press for your own blank
Looking back, win or day scuds
sunset of the chattering birds

Hidden happiness of the scene
thrown into the fortress prison
Betrayed by a friend who left, they left
Trite "this is all" fence

This is not candidate-level
don't steal your heartfelt fuel
an unusually sociable week or daybreak

If you think the secret of the scene is a cure
cast yourself into regression and whisper
"military experiment Self-blank stun play"
why hold prisoners besides me torture

Look back on what you are cautious about
fulfilled my time with harassment for sure

already worked let go of you
People often disappear for me
it makes me despair

Thrown on a powerful street
Betrayed by a friend
time and harassment
Until I can't work anymore.
Time and harassment.

We elect
so we suppose
ducked the fur annoyed have
behind her purse coldish lately

I left a child when poor warms
road to a pile of coins, my eternity
pecks around triggering bugs

worldview from a pillow's extrinsic
first thing Which hurts
If you think that hell is the cure, list
military-experimental funds will get you,
and they'll endear you neatly

Often people grow sick of whispers
pray she should vanish harboring
yes
I'm so tired of betrayal
my friends press

They're strange apologiae too,
falling back,intending revenge

Judged if respect were achieved
Why are we so tired of betrayal
felling new in red armor above soil
left to factory Group and Claims.

Dirt obeys? Must streets candor nor graves
delinquent nasty bodies assume Felicitas
an eerily quiet place for "nearby"
tired of enemy tools' betrayal

Left retaken from value of recent charm
we're not responsible for your health.
They're riding health for a pile of rocks.

Perceptual wrung out teeth
Verdict of home plan

Down-tube horror contact

need to deviate, dead raise
hands of just need regained for value,
who was kind to the World of Flying.

shallows' love diminution

Cat drawn scratch
Cave days "with" lost enthusiasm
gasp for air

Inherited heartache
Unbearable tremors

no war now
wait for history's curse on the cage

Ignored people subscribe to checks
"did they enjoy such drowned sofas"?

The funny thing is when indulgence establishes the
amount
Therefore, beating in prayer and everything "fences"
rocks and mountains, stars top in the coop

Recital that considers canard knee fur fiction

Don't be shy unravel the nanny

A priest takes care of laziness to cover
a subclass after my melancholy spell
Maintenance and approval life.

Angel of the "Lawn"

down the mattress slowly
Insult story, birds of prey
your own violence, suicide
Darkened purple veins with
morsels Legolike, rusty cough.

Impressed with rocky steps
toward departure

Took to cairns crying,
dead novel your own voice sadly
was there only controversy awaiting
your dried-out sanity, speaking
last gasp damaged the air
clashes for the summer

hills and the sea below
beaten in cheap hills and below

they find completeness in the curb
I can't.

Job Pointless Flora

badgering longing
no problem's ready at the burst

the meaning our lives can't afford

Bait

Farm props pillows, chatter inside
"Who is that talking?" Herd embarrassment
baby's crying

Disclosure: Warmth around the figures within
the house already matches diligently

They have to be surprised towards the sunset
of a provocative fountain's heart

box bonny jank of a tree's clutch

Dogs use flowers to blur flowers and remember them
the fabric twigs' ocean party confuses
worldview with the pillow inside (stomach)

Putter with gratitude like a sandy chicken
bound Sun Shelter Gray bound
when touched press heave clack

I can't wait to decide trying the witness shirt on

commit terrors with birthing
dropped as comedy baby in cold
whose impugned cries
keep private longing alive

You have to tinker with the nugget

Abuse the ground and pick up dirt
Damage the criticized cannon

Shoot down sylvan windows into "plur"
sunset talking bird given walk

slow until light broke through windshield

voices whispering in the backyard

Real-time harvest, profane harvest

swarm of hair in your head
thief's transparent claim
I love your sunflowers'
quest line dedicates their guildatures
Poke responsible safety cooperatively

Lack of resources, brass valley
Warms catharsis ice confusing sunflowers'
Stabs the pathetic mortuary
"it's growl people with babies walk in and out"
I'd suspect special friction

"worldview of bugs' triggers"
When the offscreen blast chuckles
I can't access my body's ruin, apparently joy
I pray, but I still have to raise my hand a little
Linter rodents fed extraction, paid apologies
factor
Wearing clairvoyance in dirty clothes
Trembling rice and chicken!
quote
Teen crocodiles look attractive to alcoholism
growl the milk shockproof learning

into an introvert the code jumps
Intended to take revenge

You only understood pain
Pressed dead at the sound of a button clump
smiles the trap graven corollary
knocked out
soil on teeth and fall asleep

Extracted before the anchor crystallizes
The factory smiled at its seeds
Looking up at the fun of their texture
Regained from potential value

You abandoned when you were sociable
Just to reject your foundation
For mountains and rocks
Sun Shelter Gray what I wanted to do

crawling around on the floor revolution

Worldview pillow held a guild's trumpet

ruthless combination of children and adults
ruthless

Enacted
Look

Chicken refuses made
screen screens its flying world

The teenage crocodile called Arcodontcontact
Attractive to addiction joy I can't
really access my body
pray, deviant to press

Dirty company needs
eerie quiet

Feel paid apology lint rodents
Extract and sleep "beyond" the soil
I'm going to wake up cold again

Disclosure

It's blanket tech—wrapped the numbers
of docile chickens about the wind.
I code See Them Curse
Soiled teeth and mouths
A little hand even if knocked
Raise
Kicked the animals out
of the ark

Introvert with a thousand miles of clothes
Hits and pushes people over a table of bags.

They fly to revenge
I refused
ark snoot
to Understand the mercy of a flying world
run by chickens
pain
Cut Down the Layman's Heart

Deathly sound

qualified cattle hair
Put it on your tongue and fall asleep

quaint dead sound

Anchor crystal
Light Praise Art Tension Straw Peg

moss (wilderness pocket) twigs

Extract before becoming

Intransigent
factory is out
flown into the sun
I smile guts uncovered

trap with a few words
Fun texture
look up "table to door"
Regain potential value
departing the valley its shrewdness

It was such common mountain and rock
I threw it away. Your fortune lying
the sun darts around a paltry sky
rejecting mountain and rock formations
flying worlds trained over your hills. Covered
icy pools from cold October's gray petals
still
Waiting for Trust to Fathom
to chicken out

Reject (as) impunity errors sustained duress
"feel like it's snowing"
Reject foundation

prayed-hard expertise fallen like a cat
pounced from an upset sill
global enunciated primordial fortune,
a lock of hair from your head the deed
suffering strikes
try to access the furrows of the brain "in the hut"
blind halls in wild waves' schools

allowing your turn when you're together
verboten

I think your past is safer than a consultant's
at least?
It's an undo to me that I deserve myself
the fight tells you you're tense
too tight to sleep

I can't let go of what you said earlier: "Not a cricket."
We hit each other like scapegoats
ahead of our shared sorrow
reputably tender affections whose position
flings overboard
Any pedestal to match our technocratic minutes

I think it's worse to let go than to prosper
When you think it was refactored
you tell me
as Others.
No one will show me.

why

Well frankly I won canvas
over its toiling baby window
heated from the vision of the door
went undisturbed

dimensions fat accrete from ash
enjoy your delusional food with your salt
however, family, theater, couch

Lego-like drawings
of poor Arcodontcontact
in the wild rescued by dogs.

Remember

with a minute
the day descended in putters
work meaningless flow

"if you don't"
if you can't be tough-rider's sunset go die
at the crossroads. Love and anger

Without promising pillow torture
taste your partner's closed generations
as you growl for puppetry's Reprieve!
Please give me deep spares too to suffer,
a fountain from the heart to drop a line

Depart what was left for what was once abandoned
by a Group of cairns—his own voice said?

Rusty cough morsels
Cloud scrum and classic nuggets
made pulpier and awkward and supple

Bad game sharp, functional, tired
Gun Tundra Super Infant

In the entryway to rustic footstep The Brink
In the middle of the night with ghosts and family
I was afraid in frog harbor

Nominal domination abounds can't help
it incorporates lifestyle bluff into dry air curses
Hair with grass boundaries, place of dispersal
Shave out your plenary battle
for Worried they're begging for error.

Resolve quiet domestic obituary for sky shirt
masks bed down, without your digits' play
Population feels guilty

Heavy news relics relics clout—aluminum carrier

Go beyond that with transcription services
finally "scuba diver" (converted into tubes)
open the walnuts that you face before you get old

Heaven tore the wings off my brain
cast the animals afar and rivers about
Blood nostril dragon dry-heaved

I pray for their hatred
tube vindication Horrific
World of Reason-Putter—sunlight decanter

light spare antefocus crying bread

person who repeats "let's be nice without sleeping"
very good at dismantling mystery in court

Trial diligence money grace

Reveal without problems the circuit
Perception's too slow to edit

a statue of "share" on the lawn
emasculated liege proclaims

The time limits of love balk
Spots if we keep asking
Ride Snow Fox half-damage

Balance self

Job Pointless Flora continued to evolve
no problem

Will open

warmth around
numbers slight
animals off the ark

Gray mesh up to qualified poor pockets

Lower room temperature
Bind, warm the sky of confusion
the expert panel's clutch

Somehow straw assumes a tick imbibes
water gins last time for Earth

Wingspan Biomass Moving Average

Wooden clutch box junk bonny ducks

was a party a sea of twigs of fabric
Desperate to please Sun Shelter Gray

Emergency maturity, oak tackle
If you reach the surface and can't do anything
Why do we

Should it be never?

The street
Street

Show delirium by a clock subtracting
"Closed" creepiness would be further wise
There is a tense tranquility of pacing I
Shake the enemy's tools, try to lighten them
off them Wild wave me
Shorn of drainers

Lake view and rocks from here
Red shrimp sitting to reduce tension:
The benefit of the lake in its life systems
abounds in creatures specifically chicken

Intelligence does not however systematize
where we ate beside the lake unfortunately

It can give me no thick light bulb

Gun Trundle Base Light Art Paper

Consultant pops head from stem
Refrain from windows of Sylvan stings
the flock or lack of hair on your head

Center to defeat catlike supple
Walk slowly until you forget why
Impact resistance learning failed
Waiting for the pathetic morgue
that took in my quieted comedy
for hire

Egg surprise car frame
for now you can only carry
"Egg Trowel" crash play dust

Sobbing license to evict

"Crawling on the floor,
Don't ever contact me again"
crocodile
I'm trying to write inside lately
cold invited exploitation
put on my compassion spoon
regret my time in the fortress
faint memories forgetting walked
paused or traded dry like any oak
would spend leaves season the ground
Patrol Deskant Swamp

skin loves slipping teeth
along the skeleton to meat

I'm trying to challenge and win late
because a powerhouse awaits true love

Heartfelt children pray cant and deed
Maimed or deleted "My week or day"

Find hidden happiness in the scene
double down
"on wishing"
no longer sequesters animals'
rivers lack of "in touch" turmoil
Put yourself in a bunk bed rather than
your long hair muscle around the premises
rank from the table

If you think you're cautious, the sun
winds up a literally ghostly someone
When the world blasts offscreen
laughter

Joy I can't access my body
pray, need to deviate or scrunch
your preemptive attack

all this military stun has is
unusual sociability and fuel

Take the press. Yourself let go
Once beaten to cure you can't work anymore,
the curb of hell receives pearly brains;
that brain's a worthless pearl though?

I had a snare, betrayed by a friend
I intended to take revenge
I only needed to fly into a wall

through
yet
consultancy

laughter

Recitals considered action when poor
I got shy and left. Shape war like a waffled
angry human run over by a tank
pried from the edge of the nonagonic

The public returns to it—diplomat truth mobility

so tiring to fill my time and harassments
wile dread armor's crisped fumbling,
I am our system. I know metals

Warm disclosure

Trigger confusion
lower lower lower temperature brain
For some reason wisely assume a mantic
necro-trowel off the joy received abandon

Peg Tension Straw art light

"Wingspan Biomass Moving Average" repudiation

Cubic clutch of junk

in the party fabric sea and rock coral

sun shelter unclear,
please gray blanket
huddling numbers encircled recessed!

Help helping care exhaust war
to betray anger for pride
over qualified cow hair and accents

To graze mesh run table-pocket
Maturity in a room's emergency,
Moss twigs speckle life-horarium
as moments pass through starlight?

Work on Biomass Moving Average proceeds
alike faint pink, guarding fist collapse
lighter when it reaches the surface of fabric
to touch
The warmth of the clock

Bind Vauxhall waves massive from wild
Expert panel drainer

help

heavy news

a relic of your past

deep spare guilt

Red shrimp sitting down they're so tired
Desperate to please the lake's benefits

lest they to wit the mind's workload:
"Does a bone system mill bones as numbers?"

Intelligence can't systematize graves
raw fruit squeezed from the inside
is parental juices
after all
are
the dog's brain wrong
like a bell untuned

Line Super "Front" suspension

"Enjoy your meal
It's around me, after all,
Can give a moving average delusion
of its interior when your skull
intends we rediscover death…"

forget nature walk shame
cringelike pincers surety hang ups

were wealthy and hateful
available to find love

I waited for a masochist messenger
tell whither great mastication
to do grant world security

astonished towards sunset dope,
fountains flying a cat's row of tonsils

Dog flower
Chicken chicken

provoked
Blurring flowers through him
Remembering sloppiness

Two orphan landscapes

Puttered
minutes
sky shirt
sent into the valley yard
Stem hair swarm
taped hands prayer form shape
I fell back on my head consultant

I can't wait to decide
Firmly on the farm

as the valley witnesses the shirt
Medically drop a scourge

and
kill
auric
cows

Trigger Gun Tundra Super Infant
Warm up

confusion between brains

Shoot down Knick di Mockery

Feelings pick up after dirt

a family hill's classic nugget
birds
Real-time

Can't taste
"why"
in the sewer of meaning

knowledge whelmed lawn refactored
soap
Given by honor
Kin the backyard guild me
furnishing spirit, sharpen my eye
Due diligence money blessings

Harvest contact's nuggets shot down
masochistic belfry hills confusion

Meaning fast
pierce night watch

weaponry fixates
dedicated to resource-free bring
Cooperative safety steps for din
brass diligent
warm up responsible trigger cannon

yet were the demonstrative fillers
You had to empty to tinker with bugs

Water well the last June for the ground
celebrate summer

Criticism ice damage speckled to love

Earth's quagmire
cathartic Buildings
crust

climbing diagonally
into the antechamber
For a taste
of the insect

Shake my lights loose
I'm crazy about you Crash play dust

camber

damage

Bell point made by surfing quartz wood
Awaken the place of dispersion
Suspicious fruit grips liquid hands
like your skin slips between your teeth?

You need to be indignant over climate
Ship's bell with a robe on warmth

Rattling as it cuts the icy sea
Get off first and look out, worm
twenty-five dots are like ants

Glossy watch of the lighthouse
ineffectual long no worry

I know it because I can believe it from
the construction of the planet

Backlash rate and ridicule
Talented outbreak, disconnected, cut
Willingness to see moderately the vessel
Shape the war

utensils to sliver I'm not lucky
Cruel people everyone separately
must die fate or accord
"or"
Best regards, friend

wrath of uncaring splendor however
planes life dependent on hammered flint

The theater where sky and grayness
shield your eyes

Cleavage winter days due to danger of discord
anger you gave a fingerlike vine from.

Doors of mistakes swung wide fail
toward the distant (if you win the) present
sneaking up on you yelling at your face
foolish repair

who cares
leaving the key apologies "Wretch"

Digging a ditch, feel bright red in the evening.

As it stands now, faint pink of protected fists,
coast aristocratic glum
breeze like a plaque
the strangulation of mundane vines
around into ground dirt
where families sheltered
To you to pretend they're not attractive
is to die of our own words' fear
misdirecting curiosities professionally.

Apologize as well for angry transduction games.

Forgive me. Cunning regrets spoke ridiculous fires,
Undo the best night from the suspect's room
lead him into the antechamber

Your scar from me calms the reasoning
the world hits vines against the wall.

Cruel double word
however
It is bad to borrow from the bottom of my heart
this often
to
Put yourself in using a thimble
in a perfectly messed-up ship?

As if removed, I like cried
Broken screaming end fiddles trouble
Kill until a chance comes
Please give me the rest of bull
Circus at stake in the heart of
All the tablets you cherish
time
Forgive me, you'll become a suitable tiger

you'd perform cruel pause shootings, lost measure
Tarmac analysis and conversation

blank
veil of humanity
A terrible bite's bad
worse than a left scar
Reload. Comparative violence yet
I get angry sometimes
whips. The circus lives heaven among

I can't laugh, but I'm waiting.
I feel it in my gear!

Returned

Best for

I rent in all cases
Such pop Protects
They shouldn't yell at your face like that
yell fuck your life's work
over wages "pulling relieves"
delirious garbage

Cannot abide scourges
Nor a graveyard rush rates

There's stress among prisoners between places,
expressed by the wall and the sink and drawers.
I can't say anymore.

Wasn't it cruel to imprison your corruption
in my moss ways to pillow
I could love you more for?

When you give me the truth, put it on hard
Give me as much as the truth

Cruel my senses
cruel

proper resuscitates dismantle
Cruel unknown
Catch and Release
Trust and Admiration
cramped

Betrayal old fuckler
long time no see
I rely on planet construction and lint
to make my own little precious "world"

I don't trust cruel decisions
when anyway
We Believe in good and hesitate
wry
I'm your credit, puckish
because I can commit to love
Back together, brain to brain.

Send summary value

Side panel
in which "new" films were born
beside the sun in the sky
Crash play dust
I feel like climbing diagonally
For the taste
Antechamber antechamber
Shake the light

Damage

Bell point surfing quartz wood
"collapses" assurance
A fruit grip easy to disperse
Skin, teeth meant for trouble
that'll leave a mark
I'm reversing

Do you like chances that slip their coming?

You need to be indignant at the *heat*
bang the Control Ride

Get off first and look
at the sky's garment?

The theater where dark gray hid your eyes
from me so distant I miss your eyes

Bright red orbs
Danger of discord and disconnection, cut
Willingness to see moderately.

Shaping your war blade?
Good luck, nice cow
bland farm
"crickets" muck ants
Best regards from your friends
astute as their passion
as you depart the world

The wrath of uncaring splendor
Hammering life and trouble away
Cleaving to a winter day when chance comes by

Awaken from anger and ridicule
Talent
Generate
Suspicion, liquid hands
God with no fruit
grants a finger-like vine.

It was such a mistake
They were not attractive

How the door of the squid went away
Swung towards attribution plain

Like removing from the mess of the face
a military experiment to
Inertially run as broken scream

From the line. Yelling at the plaque
Sneak up by you to commute.

I left the key oustide again, dug a ditch
felt bright red in the evening

Ship's bell on a fraught sea
Rattling out trade

As of now, faint recollections taunt
Circuses on the verge of machinery
You cherish
the pills you take
Forgive me my pink losses

aristocratic bulldozer bears down on you
the mundane vines I rent "squeeze"
passionately blamed by my own words.

Protect your fist from collapse

I apologize also for the angry transduction play,
forgive me from cunning regrets to ridiculous fires

Undo the best night from the suspect's room
From me to your net trouble

Opportunity comes and scars calm reasoning

Invading world, invading worms; vines hit the wall.

Cruel double word pleading
It's bad to borrow from the bottom, I noticed,
of my heart too often, the chocolate and plums

Put yourself in their swarm using a thimble
The perfect tip of the ship, trouble
Killing time until a chance comes

give me the rest of the bull
If you risk in the center of, you will tigress

Could perform cruel pauses yet insults

Tarmac analysis and conversation

I get angry sometimes, like a whip of fire
it's uncontrollable!
When giving
I give me as much as the truth that the truth of your
credit locked puts on me in the form of worry
itself a truth in conquest of sanity
Cruel my senses I dismantle proper resuscitation

Cruel known watches release trust

drive my clarity
dosed with houselike wings
I can't laugh, but I'm waiting.

I feel in my gear Returned to trust

Best for
I feel in all cases

They shouldn't talk to your face like that
There is no stress in the graveyard office still
Cruel people and everyone expressly separates.

A terrible bite is bad

Reload the shrine

He's not cruel when he hits
me

When
he
lies
dead

Betrayal kind of old fucks
I don't trust cruel decisions
I don't think it's good to air them
living brain to brain for fortune

prisoners sending feedback

Even to do two dopes

Orphan landscape cheerful trust and inheritance

Things like a rabbit
I hate prayer
it spells collapse lately
Radiant kernel sets for parting wishes
Comes with poster torn from scout herb stain
and for what but empty adulthood

Patrol descent wetlands that couldn't go to the
graveyard
Friends to put in the sky of the crow deer plot line

If you can't destroy anything just by folding
the stars together like a piece of paper
on a final wish of happy gray petals

I was pressed against a weak door and stumbled
Held a protracted hill with a lamb deer crow
Cancel the fate of grotesque medicine
A person who supports righteousness

Unravel the mystery in court

Perceptual, clinging share
I was hungry to love you
Where'd we forget our need? Excerpt
Sacrificial, safe tasteless dryness,
The fear of visualized connections went unfulfilled.
To protect the center of the dangerous hill
Warning to upload cliff-like barriers
crows and lambs grab the dray
in their wind, a sultry mixture of play and deceit
When
Like their wings, there is a recovery period

Incitement of yellow leaves falling

Around so many animals keep in mind
This hill and cliff won't take anymore
plunder bait from their side the virus.

why

why?

to win

Whiplash the door "pity the sun for it shines on us"
Heat from technocrat vision
Fat in the mouth in the way

What food survives you?

His own voice glues? If chicken
More than a rusty cough. Lego virulence

Cloud pulp cells mouthpiece molded scrum

If you can't be frank, you're one tough rider
Stay away from what was abandoned.
Left in your love

Please forget me *as* the next spare

Bad game sharp mouth functional, tired
Follow rustic footprints over the cairns
With ghosts and family in the middle of the night

The harbor has been laid and taken over
by our rickety ship

Cursed intersection without state, begging for error
Useless bluff the sea's chest

I lie down on the sleeping car because I put
myself under, like drowning in ill health

I can't laugh, but I'm waiting.

Hair with a mouthpiece on the border of the grass

In the wilds of breaking in hospice
Shave you off your plenary concussion:
worries without envy.

Begging for something else died in port overlay
Digital shaking
What if you did braindead
The limits of chewing in the world

Down down

Opened quietly, leaving the population
Assuming the heavenly clay wing creatures
won't imperil their intensely wicked deeds

I have smeared my hands
The smelling country has you

Snap generation
I was afraid of the situation in front of the water
where the sun did shine
Nominal domination everywhere!
What solves the article is very important
I promise to go through the world of science

If you can't make the bunker blue
difficult

For no agent
the one who
placed you in a darkened temple
connives affiliations of suffering?

Dry air

Bloody nostrils cry the dragon soggy

Know the place where life shuddered

wondering at me
Because I have to

Permission to occasion frost in time
frost of time? No good hurts to proceed

Imposing sweet escape on unfortunate painters
sober years
It looks like snow will rescue said time
in our uneventful lives
A good picture that I asked had a question
Since set, if you continue, it will be a spot:
Snorf's Deep Control Ride

For damage agents?
Cut

laughter

I'm crazy about you
No, balanced

Little Sun Ticks, Little Sun Ticks
intuit our terror
Docile flavor in A brilliant discovery

Which rear of the purchase shall be the stem

Calm in existence

barely hidden

Nocturnal attack clusterfuck

Hatred for slamming attending tragic concerns

Where even surrender has been restored
as pity

Never live again, natch

If you just hold your breath
you'll constitute a moment promise
the very barrier. Awakening
Meaning more than crying

Flattered armor did it and I convinced
Cash doesn't last a long time, yet I'm curious
if it will
blow
microplastic overhead

Light that tells you about young people
Languor as a storage room

Used today
Spin out the game

Still, how much junk is left? To flourish

When you throw me
I said "at rusty clouds," the desert
below like a dog bowl surrounded
by bags of dough depressed

The misfortune of memorization
Ashamed of canvas purgatory
High tide awaits, youthful mule.

Stick it out

Lingering around livestock for the worms
And a tunic to eat as a person

Debase emptied of confusion finally

Premonition solidification

city cooks mice and shields
Unbearable groaning mouths
Gather in a white interior with a clinking noise.
Reliable sneaky gong
Release the treasure chest and feel comfortable

Mechanical linear skyline foil
Ready for party connection

Appetite, great results
Digested hideaway from nature
Only set up to dunk, scrubness capture

Clearly admit that the crushed attunement is not a
similar friend

Operating only from deletion
Of fingers as long as they make mistakes
but pyrite's a deliberate mistake.

The truth of a better time waits upon boredom

Boredom dies
Where you can't help being.
When I met you was light
When you left night fell
If more sharpened pouch carries
broken insurers
Please forgive this misunderstanding
as trite
wallowing
around

You will be effective, your power will be doubled

Moreso with useless castration
Sweet and elegant
Your ruling
sketched
Your ruling
crib of hammers
Permitted
Faust rather than sprites commits
to wealth and adjacently intelligence
Cave system presents monetary trouble
For the promise of sundering leaves
Pride whisked a humble device made it hollow

It's a kind of a plaster soot
that fell on us in January
like we were troughed offices

all smiles to shelter better times

Side panel

Speaking of cavities that fill their journey to lace
By mistake
clench on materials "old"
must endure as "accidents"

Wait until
Holidays and your planting

Deteriorated head, worries about divorce,
Last year I made a plan for drugs. To leave.

still night = dark theater no eyes

Factoring, adaptation, rights
Do not over-participate in the hollows as a child

that mouth crazes
for your terror
Or if it makes a mistake in your curling life
later
deal

The dismantling of the buried thing is empty,
I feel uncomfortable

Who will do the best
Left behind in their travel absent device
to trial the affections set down my kindness.

The party connection shook

Road closed mesh

Full-up dictation allowance
You've worked, you'll recover.

new
Who ignores the trick

enjoy histories of drowning
armor were
Subclass after respect is achieved

If you wait for your curse
If you're a chicken priest, we'll
curb your grave
a room flush toxic

coterie adoration coterie Adoration
whose toil could get lost in mire

soft relatable Speaker
becoming a lover, chop the person's job off

What's interesting is that indulgence is always
strange
A monk buys a hand and unravels it
Subclasses following this melancholy spell

Life of mystery and approval sweet life from

It will not be released from the maintenance shop
The perfect tip of the ship, trouble
Killing time until a chance comes

Cruel double word

wages sink

Work sent pills upon a hovering tarmac
straight into the crazy mouth of the hollows

Suffocate slowly, push down the bunch
After stories of birds of prey soar

Later gasping nanny
Sandra comes to me
Insult to specs to take care of crusty April
darkening the purple veins
the sky wore.

You were impressed by rocky stairs and slipped
Establish discretion in controversy
More and more views

Just give the index a rudeness
It's our sanity and complete
Astonished. The most harmful air
covers the suction lubricant

Laziness taken care of in all cases
low hills and sea, ferrets, dogs, cats.
Chickens
a road to piles of coins, coterie my eternity

Don't take me off the roster

The novel of the dead
unsafe to pull off the shelf
Cruel everyone expressed separately.

Meet this family of cruel chickens

Cage of attention unlinks from "I can't laugh"
to
Write a letter depending on genetics

about treachery

It's love in trouble to get rid of paradox
yet when disobedience makes a profit
or betrayal, two orphan landscapes weep.
They're crazy about you?

It is not possible to disapprove from a full-fledged
eventual wish glad gray petals
Inevitably avoid the site due to their wear
Who is the air stumbled as imposition at weak door

play at the lamb deer crow grip the dray
hold the lingering hills in their wind

a machete threw the sun out
tide that draws in the drowned, starved
crush them as they take their worries away

catapult if you get lost with them every night
putting yourself up in the bloodstream helps me.
Feels like crawling on the demand for the face
Cut something deep into anger,
Petunia toss and sleep all night

When night melts, insects grow up

Someone shovels beside you
What you will stack up in time won't foment a career

Was held

I had an ounce of sugar gated around myself
Misunderstood and felt baroque
I trampled the featureless iron gate.

Nasal cup, unused laptop kitchen utensils
Infectious spokes burned hard to wire mount

wire mount

I'm hoping for their hands
income of the squirrel chasing the arrow,
Sweet light and air

Later, graffiti was detected on the suction surface.

It's the ground
Report that the buoyancy of the caper
not applied from prison
your skill is on the line. Climber

Fall or leave

blames off the mistake
I said the cloak or landing. Call out
Point out the blinking noise
that wanders through your head
Preventing you from living alone in the cave system,
So that you can see in the simplicity of your favor
Sharing breaks tremble or, ignored, cry.

If you wrap yourself in tears and a blanket,
You can pick up a piece of metal and see yourself
in the suction surface with Arcodontcontact
The crocodile
The capers will hit

Hard-working formal wear
awkward and unwieldy

Flickering
envy
victory for a committee with constant phosphorus
encircling dry beached specs.

I make time lags burn out

Like a dead chicken's world. You can cast the stack
Of a character that contains smoke and oil.

Perfection in hostility

Defend and cover up mistaken transactions
Made when there is no effort to give

That's me, the encroaching sky
playing with an annoying, falling arrow
The desk and pottery will be announced and the
marks skinned will follow. Scars stay scars

Come and put me to compassion.

Sit-down device. Quality problems
overwinter scuttled.
Vines struck the wall.

www.ingramcontent.com/pod-product-compliance
Lightning Source LLC
Chambersburg PA
CBHW071342290326
41933CB00040B/2037